A Better YOU!

A Better YOU!

CHERIE OWENS

XULON ELITE

Xulon Press Elite
2301 Lucien Way #415
Maitland, FL 32751
407.339.4217
www.xulonpress.com

© 2022 by Cherie Owens

All rights reserved solely by the author. The author guarantees all contents are original and do not infringe upon the legal rights of any other person or work. No part of this book may be reproduced in any form without the permission of the author.

Due to the changing nature of the Internet, if there are any web addresses, links, or URLs included in this manuscript, these may have been altered and may no longer be accessible. The views and opinions shared in this book belong solely to the author and do not necessarily reflect those of the publisher. The publisher, therefore, disclaims responsibility for the views or opinions expressed within the work.

Unless otherwise indicated, Scripture quotations taken from the Holy Bible, New International Version (NIV). Copyright © 1973, 1978, 1984, 2011 by Biblica, Inc.™. Used by permission. All rights reserved.

Paperback ISBN-13: 978-1-66284-674-8
Ebook ISBN-13: 978-1-66284-675-5

TABLE OF CONTENTS

Introduction vii

Different, but Alike 1
Your Purpose 7
Learning to Grow and Flourish. 11
See Yourself, Love Yourself. 17
Take a Short Rest, Then Move 19
Surround Yourself with Good People 21
"Red Flags". 25
Light in the Darkness 31
Gratitude 33
Conclusion. 37

INTRODUCTION

Becoming a better you doesn't just stop or start with yourself. Being a better you also means helping and connecting with others around you become better versions of themselves. Lay the foundation and lead the way, teach them and they may follow. They will begin to see just how abundantly happy their lives can be right alongside yours. Show compassion and care for others who may not have the strength to care and nurture themselves. You never know whose life you may have helped flourish including your own.

DIFFERENT, BUT ALIKE

Sometimes through our interactions with those we know nothing about help us figure out that we are different, yet very much alike. One interaction I had helped shine a light for me and within myself, and made me more humbled than before.

I spoke with a lady one day who was a patient of mine. She spoke about her childhood experiences and how hard it was for her growing up with it just being her and her mother. At some point in her adolescent life, the two of them struggled and they had to live out of their car for a few months. From what she felt, it was due to her mother not being strong enough to walk away from a co-dependent relationship with a man who no longer served a positive purpose in her life. It was through her journey where she found her strength at such a young age to strive for better.

I was saddened by her story but inspired by her at the same time. I, too, was once in a similar relationship where I was kicked multiple times while already at my lowest point. I wanted to leave every second of every day, but it was so hard for me to walk away from a person who I invested time with and shared a family with.

Have you heard the saying, "you'll know when you're tired and enough is enough?" Well, that day had come for me and I was scared as hell, indecisive on whether I was making the right choice or not. I found the strength, though; the strength to fight and speak life into myself until I was strong enough to leave, and I did just that.

To sum it all up, although me and this woman I cared for lived hugely different lifestyles and had different ethnic backgrounds, she Caucasian and I African American, we still shared a similar lifestyle in two different time frames. She found joy and comfort in being able to express personal things she had held in for a very long time. I was simply happy that she was happy and felt comfortable enough to share that sensitive side of her life with me.

We sometimes miss the bigger picture of how all things work together for a greater good and it starts with no judgement, just from listening to one another and although we shared similar but different stories from our past, we were still able to comfort and support each other in the present.

Encouragement to Become a Better You

- Everything is hard before it gets easy, but the journey to discovering your happiness and potential brings you to a place of a better you.
- Your mind is a powerful thing. Your thoughts and feelings create your life. Wanting better starts with you, **a better you**.
- Your journey doesn't have to end in sorrow or defeat, but it can begin with a positive mindset.
- You'll find out that you are so much more than you expected, and, in the blink of an eye, your desires will start to unfold right in front of you.

Ways to Help Yourself Become a Better You

- Try keeping a journal that only contains positive thoughts. No negativity about yourself is allowed! Write in it as often as you like: first thing in the morning, during your lunch break, right before you go to bed, once a day, once every other day, five times a day. It can be a sentence or a paragraph, just make sure they are positive thoughts about you and bettering yourself.
- **Challenge:** I challenge you for the next week to wake up every morning, look in the mirror, and say **one** positive thing about yourself. This will start your day off right. Imagine how you will feel after just one week. Think you can make it further than that? Give it a try!
- Write down four things you struggle with that you could be better at and slowly input them in your daily routine (Ex: exercise 2x week, replace soda with water, wear your favorite shade of lipstick on Mondays ect.)

1._____
2._____
3._____
4._____

YOUR PURPOSE

If you are constantly moving, you will never feel stuck. What are you being called to do? Pay attention to your intuition. As much as we try to avoid the obstacles thrown in our life, things just happen sometimes. What we don't see or pay attention to is that the outcome is always a blessing, to have grown into a mature, better experienced you.

It is not for us to get frustrated or upset at our own growth and a lot of us don't even realize that. That's what we are doing to ourselves; we are stopping our own growth. We all have a path, a purpose, and a destiny that is not and will not always be a straight and narrow path.

I began to understand that every curve for me was a lesson and a blessing in one. All those curves and brick walls changed me, but changed me for the better, and things were being revealed to me within myself that I didn't know were there.

In 2014 I made one of the biggest decisions not just in my life but my children's lives as well. I made a decision to pack up all my things and move to a new state and start fresh, it was a feeling of nervousness and excitement all at the same time. I had felt stuck for so long in my home state (Oregon) that I could no longer stand it, I longed for sunshine, warmth, and a new atmosphere. There was a need to challenge myself and know that I was capable of surviving on my own without that pillow of comfort of having my family to fall back on, so guess what? Vegas here we come!!!

Upon arrival seeing all the beautiful glowing, flashing lights actually lit a light inside of me. We stayed with an older cousin of mine for a few months while apartment hunting and I must have been way over my head. I mean three months no luck on an apartment or job, I cannot begin to explain how discouraged and defeated I felt, so much to the point I was ready to give up and move back home. Lets face it we all dread that moment that we have to go back and allow everyone to see that you failed and admit to ourselves that we were incapable of standing on our own, it was at that vulnerable moment and when all hope felt lost, I got the call back saying the apartment was available and I was approved. The joy in my heart was priceless and a month after I was hired on with a new job, finally the stability sets in, the stress is gone, and my mind is at ease and here I am several years later thriving against a brick wall that I felt had stopped me. Looking back on my journey and facing those obstacles and knowing that I am more than capable of surviving on my own in a new state, the feeling is unimaginable.

The journeys that we are on may not be the easiest, but the destination will always be the same. Everyone was put on this earth to live a happy, prosperous, abundant, and loving lifestyle. The roads and paths we face in this lifetime play a significant role in pushing us towards our destiny, as I am a firm believer that everything happens for a reason. It is all up to you and how you see and envision your own life.

I know my destiny is **great.** How are you seeing your life?

LEARNING TO GROW AND FLOURISH

When we make a sound decision to live a positive life, it also causes us to cut out and remove certain things and people from our life. Walking away and removing yourself from people and situations that mean you no good does not happen overnight. We make these decisions because we have been scarred not once, but multiple times. Most of those times it normally occurs with the ones we love and care for the most.

Learn to understand that everyone grows at their own pace. We are similar to the flowers we see on a daily basis. We are all given the same materials to help us flourish, like sun, water, and love, yet we all do not grow and flourish at the same rate, which can cause us to grow apart.

Reaching a high point in your life even when others have not does not mean that you have to stick around and endure the low vibrations of themselves or the lessons and karma that still awaits them. Remember to lower your standards for no one because the right ones will jump as high as they need to to reach you.

Putting these boundaries and standards in place means you are choosing to love yourself first and loving yourself is the best and most powerful thing you could and can ever do. That lets others know how to love you or how to better love you.

Loving Yourself

- I love myself to the moon and back, so do not come around expecting me to cut you slack.
- I love myself so much that there is no room to stay stuck.
- I understand now that I am worth more than some can ever afford or give me. It's time to get back in tune with myself and my goals.
- You can't genuinely love anything or anyone for that matter if you don't love yourself first.
- What is there to understand when one doesn't understand themselves? **Let. It. Go.**
- It is time to live! Make room for your happiness and new beginnings because they are coming. Live freely and know your worth.

Learning to Love a Better You

- What are your goals that you wish to accomplish in the future? What do you hope to strive to accomplish in the future? What do you dream of succeeding at? Whether those goals are in the near or far future, list **at least five goals** that will guarantee you becoming a better you.

1._____
2._____
3._____
4._____
5._____

- **Challenge:** Did you have a difficult day at work? Did you and a family member have an argument? Are you struggling to catch up on assignments at school? Do not let it bother you. I challenge you to begin to let things go. This challenge will not be easy, and it will take time; however, by practicing letting go of the bad and focusing on how you can make things better, you will begin your path to becoming a better, more positive you who you will love.

SEE YOURSELF, LOVE YOURSELF

*E*levation within yourself will sometimes bring conflict from others and you won't always understand why, but you have to be strong enough to set those boundaries for a new beginning and ask yourself, "Who am I, truly? Who do I see myself being in the future?" Believe in yourself and do what it takes even if it is the smallest things, for sometimes the small things matter the most.

I want nothing more than to **win!** What is it that you want? I want to **win** for myself and **win** for my family because we are all deserving of it. What I mean by **win** is; waking up scared of the struggles but still willing to face them, seeing the joy, love and smiles that I have put upon their beautiful faces, knowing that the hard work that I put in has put me in a financially free situation and mindset. Knowing that I am successful.

It's never an easy road to success, trying to reach the things we desire, but if you want it bad enough, go within, strategize, and walk the image of what you see yourself being now and in the future. Only you have control over your life's outcome, so take it by the wheel and drive like never before. It is possible and it will happen.

Guess what? It already has.

Speak life into yourself and watch it blossom like the beautiful flower you are. Your thoughts, your words, and your actions are way more powerful than you could ever know. Let no one stop you, and protect yourself at all times, for there are things out there that would love to stop you from reaching your greatness. When you love and cater to yourself like no other, that is what you will attract into your life. You are showing others how to treat and love you by loving yourself.

TAKE A SHORT REST, THEN MOVE

Life is life and things happen that we have no control over. The key is not to dwell on it or in it, but to move forward with confidence in knowing that everything will be just fine. Yes, you will have those days or even moments when you feel as though you don't know up from down, when you just don't want to do anything, and that's okay. Sometimes we need that rest for ourselves, that good old reset. Don't remain in that energy for too long, though.

There are days when I wish nothing more than to stay in my comfortable bed. I know we can all relate, but I realized that's not my end result, that's not my outcome. Where I see myself and my life, I won't be able to reach my destiny if I don't move. Remaining stagnant means you miss out on your blessings that are meant specifically for you. Well, you don't totally miss out, you just delay them because what's for you will always be for you.

Move! If you didn't hear me or feel me, I said **move!** Recite those words to yourself as many times as you need to to pull yourself out or away from whatever may be holding you back. Get a daily routine going, set your alarm, and do your best to achieve it. Make it a goal, make it a point every day to excel even with the slightest things because even a simple daily routine is a goal.

So, what do we do? We smash the hell out of that routine like **mf'n** Hulk! Wake up and claim your day every day. You are the master! You are the **mf'n boss!** Know it and understand it. You are making it and you will make it because this is your life's purpose which is to be a better higher you.

The ones who thought they were going to hold you back have another thing coming. You could care less about one's feelings, gossip, and ill intent because your priority is yourself. That, my friend, is why you will remain and continue to win.

SURROUND YOURSELF WITH GOOD PEOPLE

Succeeding and achieving comes from the great people you decide to surround yourself with. You can just call it "monkey see monkey do." We may not know at first, but the excellence within ourselves is so beautiful. It is that same excellence that we see in the amazing people we surround ourselves with that makes us strive for more.

"If they can do it, so can I." It has nothing to do with competition. Some of us just don't know our way or the path we should be on until we see the arduous work that others have put in. Even as adults, we are constantly learning every day with every step and encounter we face.

As a child I always heard the saying "It takes a village to raise a child." I find that not only to be true, but it still applies to us in our adulthood. If the village that surrounds you is determined and fighting to succeed, those are the things you pay attention to and you want to mimic that energy.

At times we may seem lost or feel as though we have gotten off track, but we must remain focused and keep our eye on the prize and understand that you are and come from a strong village, because, again, it takes a village for us to rise to our highest potential. I must say that I am immensely proud of the village I come from.

My grandfather my mother's dad, God rest his beautiful loving soul, was one of the hardest working people I know. He had been on his job for 34 years while caring for his three kids and his wife. There were several occasions where my mother and her two siblings as adults fell on hard times and had to go back home and stay with my grandfather on top of them all having their own children, a specific time when all eleven of us stayed with my grandfather and he never complained nor turned his back on us, he allowed us to all stay until our parents got back on their feet. Each sibling helping thee other watch over us wile they took turns working, as a child you don't fully understand those kind of situations until you're an adult with your own family to care for and as I got older I never understood how he did it with us all; how he was so strong, able to maintain and hold everyone up by himself but I do now, to me growing up he was my superman. Now that I have grown and walked a similar path with my own family and friends I understand what my mother always tried to explain to me that I didn't understand before, "It takes a village" she would always say even in my adult years. So even in our most vulnerable moments, sometimes "It takes a village" (family or friends) to help uplift and get you back on your feet.

"RED FLAGS"

When you've worked so hard to heal and be a better version of yourself, you ain't got time to be wasting time, and you may have to remind others of that. People who show signs of coming in and playing games would be called "red flags." Cut them off immediately and mean exactly what you say the first time.

When you start to notice peoples inconsistencies in your life, not keeping their word, you being there for them but them never for you, dumping their responsibilities off on you, only ever taking but never giving genuinely, those are red flags whether it be family or friends. Dew away with those type of people if they are not willing to change their behavior for you.

It is okay to give people the benefit of the doubt or a second chance. We are all humanly flawed, but make it a point to allow it only once because after that second time, you don't want to make it a habit of repeating yourself or to have others that don't appreciate you think that this is a revolving door that they can keep entering.

Wrap up and cut out those people who thought you couldn't stand your ground and stand by your word. As you start to grow, you will start to have a low tolerance for people's BS. Learn and master cutting those off at the head who thought they were exempt.

Daily Reminders and Efforts

- Dream so big that it outweighs the negativity of others.
- Work so hard that it outweighs your own negative thoughts.
- Open your eyes, open your mind, and <u>pay attention</u> to what the universe is showing you.
- Listen to your spark, listen to your desires, and listen to the truth inside of you.
- Follow what you know, follow the truth, and follow the reality of what's in front of you.
- Be patient. Timing is everything. Slow and steady wins the race. Remember, this is for your own protection.
- Put in the effort to love and respect yourself every day.
- Put in the effort to set those boundaries.
- Put in the effort to make your dreams a reality.
- Put in the effort for those who put in effort for you.

- Put in the effort to cleanse yourself from time to time of the negative energy (Prayer, Sage, Palo Santo ect.).
- Put in the effort to work hard for what you believe in.
- Put in the effort of having patience and understanding.
- Put in the effort to become a better you every day of your life.

Learning to Love a Better You

- Sometimes we must ask ourselves these questions:

  o Who am I?
  o Who am I surrounding myself with?
  o Do they have my best interest at heart?
  o Can you learn from them?

- **Challenge:** Greatness takes a healthy mix of effort and patience. Both can be difficult to master, but they are not impossible. Your challenge to becoming a better you is to **try**. Try your hardest at everything you do. Give 110 percent to achieve those goals you want. Fight and prove you deserve the achievement of those goals. Also try to challenge yourself to be patient with the things you normally are not. Meditate, take a walk, listen to calming music, pray, whatever it is that takes you to your inner place of peace. Patience is a virtue, and it will take patience to reach what you want in life.

LIGHT IN THE DARKNESS

While I always dreamed and prayed to work in such an amazing setting as a nurses Aid; feeding, bathing, and encouraging my patients to get stronger, letting them know this was not the end of the road they are already strong and can overcome anything, I never realized some of the concerns it would come with. Working in a hospital can be exciting and scary all at the same time. Night shifts were never my first option, but we do what works for ourselves and our families, and after two years, it became a piece of cake.

One of the most recent concerns has been the COVID-19 virus of 2020. During this time of the pandemic, the numbers became extremely high and when having to step through those doors at a critical time like this, you just never know what to expect.

One day, as I sat there trying not to let the pandemic take a toll on me, my chest began to feel tight, and all kinds of thoughts started racing through my mind. I looked out the window and all I saw was darkness with the faint glow from a streetlight.

The more I gazed at that light, I was no longer concerned or afraid. The negative thoughts were gone, and a feeling of calmness came over me. I realized at that very moment, no matter how dark things may seem, there is always a light that shines even brighter. What is it that you do whether it be your job, hobbies or things at home that warms your heart and puts a smile on your face? Whatever that may be, when you find yourself smothered with darkness, focus on the light, that thing that makes you smile, that is your light and it will always see you through the darkness.

GRATITUDE

To show the universe gratitude, I said I would complement seven people who I encountered. I didn't reach my seven, but I believe I reached one, and something much greater.

One time as I was getting my food, I saw an elderly man who needed help. As I watched him struggle getting down two steps, his wife beside him, the Spirit said to me, *don't allow him to struggle. He needs you.* Immediately I jumped out of my car, rushing past my ordered food, and I told him, "Hold on to me and I will get you there."

He looked at me and smiled. Even underneath his facemask I could see the joy on his face, and he said, "You're beautiful, you know that? A beautiful angel." I smiled back and told him how much I appreciated his complement. He asked "Do you read the Bible? Hebrews 13:2 describes you perfectly. Make sure you read it."

So, I did. I went home that night and flipped through my mobile from "You Version" Bible app until I came across Hebrews 13:2. It read:

> **"Do not neglect to show hospitality to strangers, for some have entertained Angels that you are not aware of."**

I smiled and shed a tear because although he had seen **me** as his angel, he was also **mine**. In that instance, I knew nothing could stop me; not COVID-19, not the negative thoughts of others, not even my self-doubt could stop me from my purpose. At that moment, I feared nothing because just as I told him to hold onto me and I would lead him there, a switch came on and a spark ignited within me.

As long as I keep my faith and hold onto Him, He will get me there every time no matter what. Even if I can't see the forest through the trees, He will see me through and He will do the same for you. Thank you, Scott, my angel.

Proud Moments of Self

- I am so grateful and thankful for being born as me and no one else.
- I am strong, I am wise, I am in tune, I am special, I am abundant, and I am prosperous.
- I am spiritual, I am everything, and I am love.
- I am **me** freely.

CONCLUSION

Becoming a better version of yourself and knowing who you are goes a long way, listen to your spirit they are guiding you at all times. Your purpose is to learn, teach and lead, you can't fully better yourself without the betterment of those around you. Always understand that you've always had what it takes, your smart, strong and capable.

Learn to love yourself freely without judgment and those that were only comfortable with you standing behind them tell them, "Keep your shade, I look better in the sunlight." -Cherie Owens

CPSIA information can be obtained
at www.ICGtesting.com
Printed in the USA
BVHW031007300422
635802BV00016B/697